OKAPIS

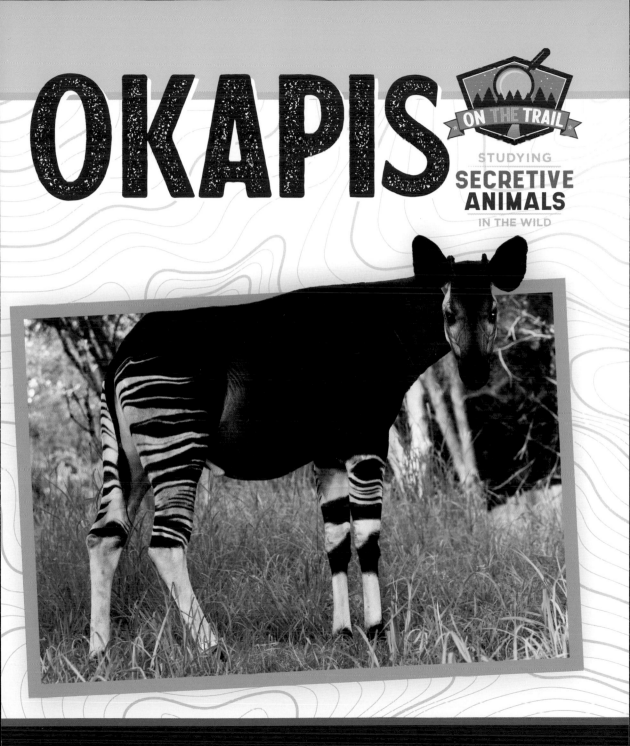

ON THE TRAIL

STUDYING
SECRETIVE
ANIMALS
IN THE WILD

CHERRY LAKE PRESS

Published in the United States of America by Cherry Lake Publishing Group
Ann Arbor, Michigan
www.cherrylakepublishing.com

Reading Adviser: Marla Conn, MS Ed., Literacy specialist, Read-Ability, Inc.
Content Adviser: John Lukas
Book Designer: Ed Morgan

Photo Credits: © Martin Harvey/Alamy Stock Photo, cover and title page; © freepik.com, TOC; © Fabian Plock/Shutterstock, 4–5; © Okapi Conservation Project, 5; © natacabo/Shutterstock, 6; Wikimedia Commons, 7 top; Wikimedia Commons, 7 bottom; © Jiri Hrebicek/Shutterstock, 8; © MarclSchauer/Shutterstock, 9; © Christopher Godfrey/Shutterstock, 10 bottom; © Dave Pusey/Shutterstock, 10 top; © Andrea Izzotti/Shutterstock, 11; © Vladimir Wrangel/Shutterstock, 12 top; © Nick Greaves/Shutterstock, 12 bottom; © Ken Schulze/Shutterstock, 13; © slowmotiongli/Shutterstock, 14; © Sarah Camille/Shutterstock, 15; © Shutterranger/Shutterstock, 16 top; © Nick Greaves/Shutterstock, 16 bottom; © Katiekk/Shutterstock, 17; © Okapi Conservation Project, 18; © Ellie Matsanova/Shutterstock, 19; Wikimedia Commons, 20; © Denis Kabanov/Shutterstock, 21; © spatuletail/Shutterstock, 22; © Okapi Conservation Project, 23; © Olena Tselykh/Shutterstock, 24; © clayton harrison/Shutterstock, 25; Jiri Hrebicek/Shutterstock, 26–27; © Mia2you/Shutterstock, 28; © spatuletail/Shutterstock, 29; © Nadezhda Shoshina/Shutterstock, 31.

Cherry Lake Press is an imprint of Cherry Lake Publishing Group.

Library of Congress Cataloging-in-Publication Data

Names: Markovics, Joyce L., author.
Title: Okapis / by Joyce L. Markovics.
Description: First edition. | Ann Arbor, Michigan : Cherry Lake Publishing,
   [2021] | Series: On the trail: studying secretive animals in the wild |
   Includes bibliographical references and index. | Audience: Ages 10 |
   Audience: Grades 4-6
Identifiers: LCCN 2020030357 (print) | LCCN 2020030358 (ebook) | ISBN
   9781534180482 (hardcover) | ISBN 9781534182196 (paperback) | ISBN
   9781534183209 (ebook) | ISBN 9781534181496 (pdf)
Subjects: LCSH: Okapi—Juvenile literature.
Classification: LCC QL737.U56 M375 2021 (print) | LCC QL737.U56 (ebook) |
   DDC 599.638—dc23
LC record available at https://lccn.loc.gov/2020030357
LC ebook record available at https://lccn.loc.gov/2020030358

Printed in the United States of America
Corporate Graphics

CONTENTS

OKAPI MISSION

The year was 1987. U.S. **zoologist** John Lukas stepped off an old cargo plane. He had just arrived in Zaire, a country that's now called the Democratic Republic of Congo. And John still had seven tough days of traveling ahead of him. He had come all the way to Africa to learn more about a strange and secretive animal—the okapi (oh-COP-ee).

The Congo River in the Democratic Republic of Congo

LOOK CLOSER

An okapi is about the size of a horse and stands about 6 feet (2 meters) tall. It can stretch its neck another 2 feet (61 centimeters)!

John had only ever seen an okapi in a zoo. The creature fascinated him. For one thing, an okapi has extraordinary markings. It has stripes like a zebra and a neck and ears more similar to a giraffe. And the okapi has a dark blue tongue that's so long it can lick its own eyes! "It has amazing **biology**," John says. Yet little was known about okapis in the wild because they're seldom seen.

Zoologist John Lukas with an okapi

RECENT
DISCOVERY

Wild okapis only live in one place in the entire world—the Congo River **basin** in the heart of Africa. They're often found within the Ituri (ee-TOOR-ee) Forest. The **native** people who live in the dense rainforest have known about okapis for thousands of years. However, scientists first learned about the **elusive** animals just a little over 100 years ago.

The native people of the Ituri Forest are known as the Mbuti (em-BOO-tee) Pygmies. Most Pygmy people are less than 5 feet (1.5 m) tall.

In 1901, an explorer named Harry Johnston went searching for the okapi, or the "African donkey" as it was called at the time. With the help of native guides, he explored the Ituri Forest. Finally, he found some okapi tracks in the mud under a thick **canopy** of trees. Yet Harry never saw a live animal. He did collect an okapi skin and skull. Eventually, the bones helped scientists **classify** the new animal as the only living relative of the giraffe.

Strips of okapi skins collected by Harry Johnston

An illustration of an okapi based on a painting by Harry Johnston

LOOK **CLOSER**

Harry Johnston is credited with discovering the okapi. As a result, the animal's scientific name is _Okapia johnstoni_.

FOREST GIRAFFE

When John Lukas finally reached the Ituri Forest, he understood why okapis are known as forest giraffes. Okapi **habitat** is so thick with trees and other plants it's almost impossible for a person to walk through. Little sunlight can **penetrate** the leafy canopy. Also, rain frequently falls. Amazingly, okapis are perfectly adapted to their forest home.

An okapi in its forest home

Okapis have soft, reddish-brown fur that blends in with the forest. Their fur is also oily. So when it rains, water slides right off their bodies and the animals stay dry. On their legs and backsides, okapis have bold, zebra-like stripes. "These markings provide amazing **camouflage**," says John. When the sun shines through the canopy, it creates strips of light on the forest floor. The light looks like the stripes on okapis' bodies. As a result, "they are very difficult to see," says John.

Okapi fur is so soft "it feels like velvet," says John.

LOOK **CLOSER**

Like a fingerprint, each okapi has a unique stripe pattern. Baby okapis use the stripes to recognize their mothers.

SPECTACULAR SENSES

Okapis are so hard to spot that John never saw one during his first trip to Africa. He has seen them on other **expeditions** to the Ituri Forest—but not without great effort. Beyond their camouflage, okapis have ears that can pick up the slightest sounds. "Like a giraffe, the ears are large and can move independently," says John. This allows them to hear approaching humans and **predators**, such as leopards, from all angles.

Okapis can pick up sounds made by other okapis that neither humans nor predators can hear.

Leopards are the main natural predators of okapis. Okapis can fight off leopards by kicking them with their strong legs.

Okapis can also smell an enemy from far away, giving them time to hide in the thick underbrush. In addition, they sniff the ground for traces of other okapis. Most of the time, okapis live alone, and each animal has a home range. To mark their **territory**, okapis have **scent glands** on each foot. As they walk, the glands produce a sticky, tarlike liquid that tells other okapis, "I live here, move it!"

A male okapi patrolling his territory

LOOK CLOSER

A female okapi's territory is about 1.9 square miles (5 square kilometers), while a male's is 4.6 square miles (12 square kilometers).

LEAFY DIET

These incredible animals also use their excellent sense of smell to find food. "Okapis eat leaves, fruit, and **fungi**," says John. "They eat as many as 100 species of plants, many of which contain **toxins**." John has seen okapis consuming clay in the soil and burned wood, which help detoxify the leaves. The animals are careful not to eat too many leaves from any one plant to limit the amount of toxins.

An okapi eating leaves

Okapi droppings

An adult okapi can eat an astounding 40 to 65 pounds (18 to 29 kilograms) of leaves each day! Okapis use their long **prehensile** tongues to strip leaves and buds off tree branches. As they browse for food, they **prune** the forest, sometimes creating a noticeable line in the greenery. As a result, John thinks of okapis as animal gardeners.

Okapis use their tongues for grooming their fur as well.

LOOK **CLOSER**

Okapis are most active during the afternoon and evening.

BABY
OKAPIS

John saw that male and female okapis live alone in the forest most of the time. Each year, they come together to **mate**. Females tell males they're ready to mate by making special sounds below the hearing range of most animals and people. Males stretch their necks, lift their back legs, and circle females before mating. After 14 to 16 months, females give birth to a single baby called a calf.

Female okapis are often larger than males. Males have skin-covered horns called ossicones that point backward.

Calves look like tiny adults. They can stand soon after birth. For the first 6 to 9 weeks, the babies stay in one place called a nest. Mothers check on and feed their babies often. "Most newborn animals **defecate** within 12 hours of birth," says John. "But okapis hold their stool for 60 days, to avoid giving leopards a scent and a chance to find them."

Calves will nurse from their mothers for 8 months.

LOOK CLOSER

Mother and baby okapis communicate with each other using unusual calls that predators can't hear. Scientists use special technology to record okapi sounds. "It's quite dinosaur-like when boosted to our hearing range," John says.

ELEPHANT HIGHWAYS

"Okapis are entirely dependent on their forest home," says John. They're also dependent on giants that share the Ituri Forest—elephants! As the huge elephants walk through the forest and feed, they stomp on plants and knock over trees. "Elephants make highways through the forests," he says. This in turn helps create open walkways for okapis and other animals, making it easier for them to find food. The clearings also encourage the growth of young trees on which okapis feed.

Okapis and elephants live peacefully side by side.

Elephants shake trees to knock down fruit to eat. Then they spread the seeds of the fruit in their droppings.

However, the future of Ituri Forest elephants is at risk. Hunters looking for valuable ivory tusks are **poaching** elephants at an alarming rate. As a result, there are nearly 80 percent fewer elephants in the forest than there were 20 years ago. This is having an impact on okapis' access to food.

These feet are from elephants killed by poachers. Poachers have been known to hurt people in order to get elephant ivory.

MAJOR THREATS

Another major threat to the okapis and other forest animals is habitat loss. Thousands of people live in and around the Ituri Forest. Some cut down and burn the trees to create farmland. Others enter the forest to mine for gold and diamonds. Digging mines destroys the land and the plants that okapis depend on. What's worse, miners sometimes kill okapis and other wildlife for food.

Gold mining in the Ituri Forest

Okapis are also threatened by **civil war** in the Congo. Over many years, different groups of people have been fighting for control of the land and its resources. Desperate people escaping the warfare have turned to the forest for safety. This has led to a sharp increase in logging and poaching of okapis. In the last 25 years, okapi numbers have dropped by over 50 percent.

Peacekeeping soldiers in the Congo

LOOK **CLOSER**

Okapis are an endangered species, which means they're at risk of dying out.

OKAPI
WILDLIFE
RESERVE

In 1992, John teamed up with **conservation** organizations and the Congolese government to create the Okapi Wildlife Reserve (OWR) in the Congo. The reserve protects one-fifth of the Ituri Forest, including prime okapi habitat. John also led a team to set up an educational center to study okapis.

The Okapi Wildlife Reserve

In 2012, poachers attacked the Okapi Wildlife Reserve. They burned down buildings and killed six staff members and 14 okapis. The OWR faced another deadly attack in 2017.

Because tracking and studying okapis in the wild is so tough, John decided to safely capture some animals to study and breed. He placed them in a large enclosure that **mimicked** their natural habitat. John and other scientists closely watched the animals, gathering important data about their behavior. He and his team also set up cameras in the forest to observe okapis in their natural home.

An okapi in an enclosure at the OWR

SPREADING THE WORD

Any efforts to protect okapis need the support of the local people, says John. So he started the Okapi Conservation Project (OCP) to not only preserve okapi habitat but also educate and help villagers. OCP trains them to become caretakers of the forest. This benefits the okapis and provides the people with much-needed income. The OCP also teaches villagers new farming methods that don't harm the environment. "More trees mean more okapis," John says.

Okapis are an important symbol of the Democratic Republic of Congo, says John.

John feels strongly that children should be educated about okapis too. "Kids are our future," he says. "After learning about okapis, children bring what they learn home." And when they value these special animals, they want to protect the places where they live. So John and the OCP team created World Okapi Day, especially for children in the Congo. During the celebration, kids can win prizes, such as free schooling and school supplies.

John with Ituri Forest villagers

LOOK CLOSER

The OCP also provides funding for new schools and health clinics in the Congo.

ZOOS

Zoos around the world support John's work with okapis. Many have their own okapi exhibits. In fact, around 180 okapis live in zoos worldwide. Most okapi exhibits are designed so guests can look at the shy animals without disturbing them. Thanks to these exhibits, people can glimpse a beautiful animal they would never be able to see in the wild.

People observing an okapi in a zoo exhibit

For John, zoos are also important conservation partners. Many have successful breeding programs. Raising okapis in zoos is a way to ensure the survival of the species. And zoos help spread awareness about okapis and their conservation. However, John's main focus is the Ituri Forest and the okapis and people who live there.

An okapi mother nursing her calf in a zoo

LOOK **CLOSER**

John usually travels to the Congo three to four times year. When he's not in the Congo, he manages the OCP from an office provided by the Jacksonville Zoo and Garden in Florida.

MOVING FORWARD

Despite setbacks and challenges, John works around the clock to help save okapis and their homeland. With help from many people, OCP was able to rebuild all the structures damaged in the 2012 attack on the Okapi Wildlife Reserve. John is determined to expand the reserve's center. And he continues his efforts to help communities live **sustainably** in the forest.

John is also trying to encourage the Congolese government to protect all areas where okapis are found and to make conserving okapis a national movement. "I don't have much time left, so I'm going to spend every moment trying to make a difference," he says.

LOOK CLOSER

It's thought that only about 10,000 to 20,000 okapis remain in the wild today.

FAST FACTS

OKAPIS

Scientific Name
Okapia johnstoni

Physical Description
Reddish-brown fur with black-and-white striped front and back legs

Size
Up to 6 feet (2 m) tall

Weight
500 to 800 pounds (227 to 363 kg)

Main Diet
Leaves, fungi, and fruit

Habitat
Congo River basin in the Democratic Republic of Congo

Life Span
20 to 30 years

REPUBLIQUE DU BENIN
POSTES 1996

Okapia johnstoni

135f

DID YOU KNOW?

- Like giraffes, okapis splay, or spread, their front legs to reach the ground to drink water.

- An okapi's tongue is a great grooming tool. It helps keep the animal's fur clean and soft.

- Okapi calves weigh about 35 pounds (16 kg) at birth.

- Okapis make many different sounds to communicate. In addition to the low sounds that people can't hear, they whistle, bleat, and cough.

GLOSSARY

basin (BAY-suhn) an area of land around a river from which water drains into the river

biology (bye-AH-luh-jee) the basic important activities performed by an animal in order to be alive

camouflage (KAM-uh-flahzh) a natural coloring or marking that allows an animal to hide by blending in with its surroundings

canopy (KAN-uh-pee) the top layer of leaves and branches covering a forest

civil war (SIV-il WOR) a war between people of the same country

classify (KLAS-uh-fye) to put into a particular group based on shared characteristics

conservation (kahn-sur-VAY-shuhn) the protection of wildlife and natural resources

defecate (DEF-ih-kayt) to have a bowel movement

elusive (ih-LOO-siv) very hard to catch or find

expeditions (ek-spuh-DISH-uhnz) long trips taken for a specific reason, such as exploring

fungi (FUHN-jye) plantlike organisms that have no flowers or leaves and grow on other plants

habitat (HAB-ih-tat) the natural home of an animal or plant

mate (MATE) to come together to have young

mimicked (MIM-ikd) copied

native (NAY-tiv) a person or animal belonging to a particular place

penetrate (PEN-uh-trate) to go inside or through

poaching (POH-ching) hunting illegally on someone else's land

predators (PRED-uh-turz) animals that hunt and kill other animals for food

prehensile (pree-HEN-sil) adapted for grasping or taking hold of something

prune (PROON) to cut off branches from a tree or bush

scent glands (SENT GLANDZ) body parts that give off a liquid with a strong smell

sustainably (suh-STAYN-uh-blee) living in a way that does not harm the environment

technology (tek-NAH-luh-jee) equipment developed from and used for science

territory (TER-uh-tor-ee) the area where an animal lives and finds its food

toxins (TAHK-sinz) poisons

zoologist (zoh-AH-luh-jist) a scientist who studies animals

READ MORE

Antill, Sara. *Okapi*. New York: Windmill Books, 2011.

Ganeri, Anita. *The Story of the Okapi*. Chicago: Heinemann Library, 2016.

Wojahn, Rebecca Hogue, and Donald Wojahn. *A Cloud Forest Food Chain*. Minneapolis: Lerner Publications, 2010.

LEARN MORE ONLINE

Jacksonville Zoo and Garden: Okapi
https://www.jacksonvillezoo.org/okapi

Okapi Conservation Project
https://www.okapiconservation.org

San Diego Zoo: Okapi
https://animals.sandiegozoo.org/animals/okapi

Zoo Berlin: Okapis
https://www.zoo-berlin.de/en/species-conservation/worldwide/okapis

INDEX

ABOUT THE AUTHOR

Joyce Markovics has authored more than 150 books for young readers. She's wild about rare and unusual animals and is passionate about preservation. Joyce lives in an old house along the Hudson River in Ossining, New York. She would like to thank John Lukas for his generous contribution to this book and to the okapis and people of the Congo.